Praise for *Cultivating The Garden Within*

"This book has a delightful clarity and lightness. If you take the time and open your mind, you will be introduced to concepts that can change your life."

Jennifer Louden
Bestselling Author of *The Woman's Comfort Book*

"Anyone seeking an insightful guide for growing their own 'human bean' will enjoy this accessible, humorous 'how-to' book."

Ann Cheng
Master Certified Coach

"Every gardener knows the pleasure and satisfaction of a plant in first bloom: planted, nurtured, pruned, watched over, and cared for. Imagine the result of that attention to our lives ... and the possibilities! Using the metaphor of gardening, this book provides the steps to improve your life."

David Slover
Sales Manager

"With refreshing humor, this little book provides guidance to improving both your garden and your life — a lovely departure from the abundant traditional 'self-help' books."

Dr. Renata Soulen
Professor of Radiology, Wayne State University

"I love it. It is whimsical and yet has so much great information. The book will make a wonderful gift to share with my friends."

Mary Ann Pate
Productivity Consultant, A Timely Solution

"A lighthearted approach for those who want to be the most they can be in the garden of their own life."

Kathryn DeSilva Vigar

Cultivating The Garden Within

Your Guide to Living A Richer Life

Bonnie Keast, Ed. D.
C. L. Haney

Illustrated by C. L. Haney

Earthsong Voices
San Ramon, California
www.EarthsongVoices.com

Copyright © 2004 by Bonnie Keast and C. L. Haney
Cover and internal design © 2004 by Earthsong Voicess

All rights reserved. No part of this book may be reproduced in any form, or by any electronic or mechanical means including information storage and retrieval systems — except in the case of brief quotations embodied in critical articles or reviews — without written permission from its publisher, Earthsong Voices.

Published by Earthsong Voices
San Ramon, California
www.EarthsongVoices.com

First Printing 2004
Second Printing 2009, revised
ISBN: 0-9749111-1-9

Printed and bound in the United States of America

Bonnie and C.L. dedicate this book to gardeners and soul growers everywhere who are willing to dig in their own soil in order to experience a greater sense of beauty in both their outer and inner worlds.

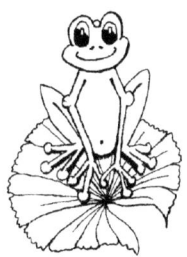

Bouquets

Just as the garden frequently rewards us with bouquets of flowers and baskets of vegetables, so friendships also provide unique gifts. As we were working on our book, we found many friends and associates who helped us grow *Cultivating The Garden Within*. They believed in us, applauded our efforts, and encouraged us throughout the long growing process. They know who they are, and we are deeply grateful to each of them for their support.

We also had a group of friends who helped us dig deeper in the garden. With their assistance, suggestions, and critiques they enabled us to imagine possibilities we hadn't grasped, find errors we didn't know we'd made, and believe in potentials we hadn't dreamed. We've gathered showers of flowers and present them with gratitude to Ann Cheng, Ken Cook, Michael Doyle, Lynn Fernandez, Sue Fordon, Susanna Gordon, Linda Hanson, Drene Johnson-Morrow, M. A. Klein, Karen Leffler, Rick Lumsden, Tia Marshall, Terry McDonald, Shamahl Nolan, Roberta Ryan, Trudy Schoneman, Howard Shattner, David Slover, Rony Soulen, Donna Van Stralen, Kathryn Vigar, and Steve Whiteford.

Finally, we offer a big bouquet to our editor, Cathlin Davis. Her bouquet is the one tied with a special, red-penciled bow.

Contents

A Note to our Reader xiii
Foreword xv
The First Gardens xvii

Section One: Designing 1

Designing the Garden Outside 3

Designing Life or Walking Through It? ...11
  Taking Charge of your Life

What Do You Value? 17
  Honoring Yourself

How Do You See It? 25
  Perception Determines Action

What's Your Reaction Pattern? 31
  Responding On Auto-Pilot

Section Two: Planting 39

Planting the Garden Outside 41

What Do You Mean, Practice? 47
  Planting Habits

Whom Do You Trust? 53
  Sustaining Relationships

What Are You Nipping in the Bud? 59
  Timing Is Critical

What Mood? 65
  Tilling Your Emotional Soil

SECTION THREE: TENDING 73

Tending the Garden Outside 75

Taking Care of Basics? 81
BREATHING AND OTHER NECESSITIES

Routine? What Routine? 87
CULTIVATING USEFUL SYSTEMS

Is It Time to Let Go? 93
WEEDING YOUR RELATIONSHIP GARDEN

Do You Hear That Voice? 99
TRAINING YOUR INNER VOICE

SECTION FOUR: ENJOYING 107

Enjoying the Garden Outside 109

What's Worth Celebrating? 115
FUELING YOUR ENTHUSIASM

What Shows on Your Face? 121
REVEALING YOUR EMOTIONAL LANDSCAPE

How Do You Define Success? 127
CONDITIONS OF SATISFACTION

How Often Do You Pause To Refresh? ..133
GRATITUDE FERTILIZES

RESOURCES 143

Cultivating The Garden Within

Little by little we have lost our sense of belonging. We long for intimacy but we can no longer achieve it. We live with an increasing sense of loneliness. Entangled in efficiency, we have forgotten why we want to be efficient in the first place. We have become wonderfully efficient beings who do not have time to care either for the earth's garden or for the garden of our souls.

Julio Olalla, Founder of Newfield Network

INTRODUCTION

A NOTE TO OUR READERS

This book is yours, and as reader and explorer, you may use it in any number of ways. The book is not sequence-dependent, although you may want to read it from beginning to end. You also could simply scan the chapters and read only the subjects of interest.

Time is a precious commodity. Therefore, the information sections in *Cultivating The Garden Within* are brief, condensed versions of personal development. At the back of the book you'll find a list of book references that provide more extensive information on various topics.

A short exercise follows each information section to help you become more aware of yourself and how you interpret your world. Following each exercise is a space for notes. The NOTES page begins with questions. You could choose to write answers to one or more of the questions, ignore the questions altogether and write about something else related to your thinking, or not write any notes at all.

Following the Notes is a section entitled DIGGING A LITTLE DEEPER. This contains another exercise or activity related to the topic. Again, read through the task to see if it is something you are curious about. You may want to do the activity, try to answer the questions, or merely consider possibilities the activity presents.

However you choose to use this book, we encourage you to look at gardens, both those outside and those inside us, through new eyes. May your gardens flourish!

INTRODUCTION

Foreword

The act of gardening involves planning, planting, and tending. Having decided to keep a garden, the gardener becomes committed to a never-ending round of work. In addition to the expected designing of what goes where, preparing the soil, planting, watering and weeding, there are always the unexpected challenges. Weather conditions, insect infestations, and plant disease each demand attention.

There is no "instant gratification." Rather, a garden provides an on-going sense of satisfaction as challenges are met and plants grow and take shape, develop in surprising ways, and often, just when you thought they had died completely, spring back to life.

So, too, it is when cultivating the "garden within." Finding the space in our busy days and weeks to focus on our inner selves is challenging. Finding and accepting who we are, nourishing our inner life, discarding old habits that no longer serve us and developing new habits all take time. Yet, by becoming more intimate with ourselves, we can increase our sense of personal success and grow more and more attuned to the rhythms of our own natures. As we take the time to observe ourselves in action at work, with our families, and with our friends, we begin to notice what is nourishing us and what is stunting our growth. Becoming more intimate with ourselves enables us to bloom and grow in new and often surprising ways.

Come, enter and explore the gardens ...

Introduction

The First Gardens

Gardens first appeared as early man grew tired of wandering in search of food and settled down to cultivate the land. These first gardens were simple enclosures meant to keep livestock and plants in, and wild animals and other marauders out.

From these humble beginnings, several philosophies of gardening evolved. In the East, gardens were conceived as spaces for solitary reflection and meditation, where one could connect to sources and spirits of the natural world. In the Greco-Roman view, by contrast, gardens served as a backdrop to socialization and the pursuit of relaxation and pleasure. And in Western monastic tradition, gardens functioned as places of religious contemplation and practical work, where plants were cultivated for medicinal and culinary purposes.

Happily, modern gardens draw inspiration from all these early examples. Today, a garden can be a whimsical playground, a calm haven, an abundant source of food, a lively entertainment area, a beautiful adjunct to a house, or all of the above!

SECTION ONE

DESIGNING

"Everybody needs beauty as well as bread,
places to play in and pray in, where
Nature may heal and cheer and give
strength to body and soul alike."
John Muir

Designing the Garden Outside

So you want to grow a garden. Congratulations! You are in for a rewarding experience, but where do you start? It can seem intimidating at first.

To transform a plot of ground into a living, breathing, growing place, you first need to decide what kind of garden you want. Second, you need to understand the space where you will plant it.

Many of us, enthusiastic and optimistic, bypass these critical preliminaries, and head straight for our local nursery. We select plants on whim and return with a triumphant assortment of annuals, perennials, and shrubs, which may or may not do justice to our ultimate goal or to our growing space.

If, instead, we take a little time to visualize and prepare, our garden will more likely meet our expectations. In fact, gardening is just as much an exercise for the mind as it is for the senses. A garden begins in our imaginations.

Dreams

What kind of garden, then, do you envision? Perhaps you dream of a peaceful, secluded retreat from which to escape the demands of a hectic day-to-day life. Or maybe you want a large, open area for recreation and entertaining with a wide deck, pool, and children's play area. You may be looking for a spot to grow vegetables or a place to putter. Perhaps you are interested in creating a habitat for butterflies, hummingbirds, or maybe even deer! You may simply want more privacy from a neighboring house or street noise, or minimal yard maintenance. Whatever your reasons are, write them down.

DESIGNING

REALITIES

After you've decided your purpose, look at what you have to work with. What does nature offer? A good rule of (the green) thumb is that it's easier to work with nature than against it.

Since plants grow best in conditions that mimic their native climates, an accurate evaluation of your garden's conditions can make the difference between a garden that flourishes and one that ... well, doesn't.

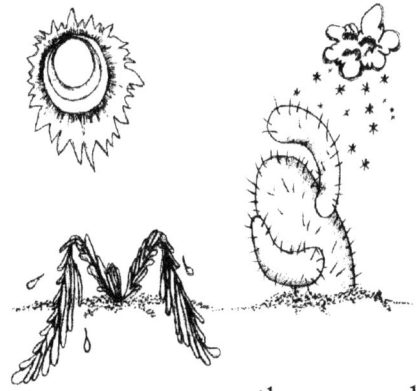

Climate, sun exposure, soil type, and garden dimensions all play a part in a successful garden design. To learn more about your particular natural conditions, ask a neighbor or your local nursery, or consult one of the many excellent gardening books on the subject.

5

Plans

Putting together the dream with the reality allows the gardener to bring the personality of the landscape to life. Like most of gardening, it is a repeating process. Recognizing the existence or lack of a particular resource may prompt a revision of planned purpose, and vice versa.

The planning stage allows you as gardener to become an artist, painting the canvas of your garden space with trees, shrubs, and ground cover.

Put your plan in writing. Or rather, in drawing! First lay out the boundaries of your garden space on a piece of graph paper. Outline existing structures, primary areas of use, and major features such as shade trees or lawn area.

Next, pencil in the foundation planting that will shape the space. Foundation plantings are those trees and shrubs that form the permanent background of your garden. Conifers, broad-leaved evergreen trees and shrubs, ferns, and hardy perennials offer many options for the "bones" of your garden.

Now add the transitions, usually flowering shrubs and perennials, which create interest for a season or two, then die back or stop blooming to allow other plants to take center stage. Last come the accents, the brief bursts of color that come from bulbs and short-blooming flowering plants.

As you design, keep in mind the essential elements that every good artist considers: scale, repetition, and pattern. Also think abut a balanced contrast in height, texture, and color.

Choose a color palette that pleases your eye. Your palette may contain many colors or only one. An all-white garden, for example, can be lovely. The palette may even echo the colors of your home's interior. Select plant types that appeal to you, either for their looks, texture, or scent.

There are no rights and wrongs when it comes to color and form. When in doubt, however, err on the side of simplicity. Busy details are often lost as a garden grows, and can make you crazy, especially once you get to the planting!

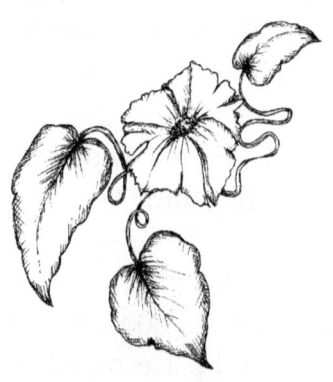

DESIGNING

Thinking about your purpose, knowing your soil and growing conditions, and drawing concrete plans are important steps in designing the garden in your yard. There's also a vast garden within each of us to design.

        Come, enter the garden within ...

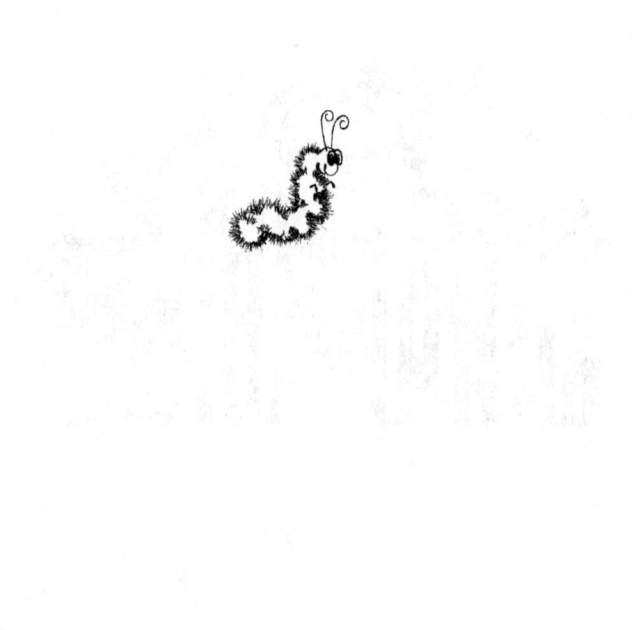

Gardens begin in our imaginations.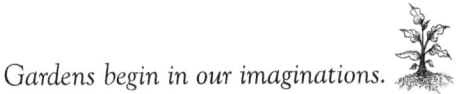

Designing Life or Walking Through It?
TAKING CHARGE OF YOUR LIFE

A garden can be designed from the ground up. Many of us do not realize that we also continually design our own lives, either consciously or unconsciously. Most of us desire a life that satisfies both our needs and our wants. For us, a satisfying life means finding pleasure, nurture, fulfillment, and gratification within our family, in our careers, in our friendships, and in our leisure activities.

For some people, life just seems to happen. Events occur and they react. They feel lucky or unlucky about the way the events unfold. In fact, much of their life force seems to be spent reacting to what's going on around them rather than having a clear sense of purpose about their actions and knowing what they truly care about.

Other people know what they care about; they establish priorities, they have goals, and they make plans to meet those goals. Just as the garden designer begins with a dream and an analysis of the available space, these people take an active role in designing their lives.

They look at their values, at the skills they've developed, and at the activities they enjoy as places to begin. They dream of possibilities and analyze their current life situation and themselves. Although there are always surprises and detours (this is LIFE, after all), having a design helps them achieve greater satisfaction.

Just as gardeners change the landscape by design, all of us can create different patterns of living and being to gain greater pleasure and delight in our lives. As humans, we have the capacity to reflect, analyze, and learn. We do so in order to shape our lives and come closer to our dreams.

Designing

During the planning stage, a gardener looks at the existing area. What is the size and shape of the space? What plants are already there? What is the soil composition? What is the topography? How much effort might be required to make major changes?

The following exercise gives you an opportunity to look at the shape of your current life and decide your level of satisfaction with each listed area.

Pick a Number

Look at the list. Define each life area in ways that make sense for you. Put a number in the first column beside each area. One (1) means not satisfied at all and ten (10) means you don't see how it could be better.

Work/Career ___ ___
Money ___ ___
Health/Fitness ___ ___
Friends ___ ___
Family ___ ___
Relationship/Significant Other ___ ___
Personal/Spiritual Growth ___ ___
Fun/Recreation ___ ___
Physical Environment ___ ___
Intellectual Stimulation ___ ___
Sense of Security ___ ___
Emotional Well-being ___ ___
Social Life ___ ___
Other _____ ___ ___

Now go back to the same areas, and in the second column put a number that represents your ideal score in that area. For instance, if you are scoring your physical environment and feel that currently it's a 5, but physical environment isn't all that important in your life, you might give it an ideal score of a 5 or a 6.

Notes

What did you notice as you did the two sets of scoring? Was one of them (current or ideal) easier to do? Do you know the reasons you decided on the number you chose? What's missing for you that would have made a number higher?

 ### Digging a Little Deeper

Look at the likenesses and differences between your current scores and your ideal scores. If you're like most people, you'll find some areas of your life are quite satisfactory. In some areas there may be large discrepancies between your current and ideal scores, in other areas none. You'll also notice there are areas you don't care much about at the present time.

Pick one area you'd like to move closer to your ideal. What would it take to move up by one or two points?

Are you currently willing and able to do it?

Is there time in your schedule to make the desired changes?

Right now, write on a calendar or in your planner what you will do and when. Be sure to plan enough time to complete your proposal.

What kind of a garden,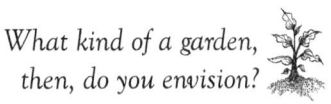
then, do you envision?

What Do You Value?
Honoring Yourself

In gardening as in life, it helps us to know why we are doing something. Perhaps we plan a garden because we like to dig in the earth. Or maybe it is because we like to watch the changes taking place through the seasons. Or we may want a garden simply because we like the flowers, or vegetables, or greenery growing there.

As humans, so often we move and behave automatically. Yet when we know our own core values and have a sense about how and why we are doing things the way we are doing them, we have much greater power to grow and change. Asking the question, "For whom am I doing this?" or "For the sake of what am I doing this?" is a very important action when designing the various areas of our life.

Often we get into habits of doing things in certain ways or doing things that made sense at one time, but no longer benefit our current aims or us.

For instance, many of us write out "To Do" lists to help keep track of our obligations and our desires. There's satisfaction in being able to check off errands and activities as they are accomplished. However, do we know how this particular task fits with our short and long range intentions, and with our current commitments?

Taking time to think about our life in the bigger sense makes all the necessary moment-to-moment decisions more effective. When we know what is most important to us, we can keep moving through the tumbles of life.

Designing

When designing a garden, the space, topography, climate, and purpose all play their part. As you design the next phase of your life, the following exercise will give you an opportunity to reflect on what you care about most.

Connecting to Values

STEP ONE: Look at the entire list of 40 values on the next page. You may define each in a way that makes sense to YOU and add anything you feel is missing. Think about each value.

- Put a check beside the ones that fit you.
- Put an x beside those that don't feel like you at all.
- Put a question mark beside any that aren't definite "fits" or "doesn't fit".

Go slowly and don't rush. Use your intuition and notice what calls to you.

Values

- __ Achievement
- __ Advancement
- __ Adventure
- __ Aesthetics
- __ Affiliation
- __ Authority
- __ Balanced Lifestyle
- __ Challenge
- __ Change/Variety
- __ Competence
- __ Competition
- __ Creative Expression
- __ Economic Reward
- __ Expertness
- __ Family
- __ Fast Pace
- __ Financial Security
- __ Health/Fitness
- __ Honesty
- __ Influencing People
- __ Intellectual Stimulation
- __ Leadership
- __ Learning
- __ Location
- __ Personal Growth
- __ Physical Challenge
- __ Precision Work
- __ Prestige
- __ Quality
- __ Recognition
- __ Responsibility
- __ Risk Taking
- __ Safety
- __ Security
- __ Self-Direction/Autonomy
- __ Self-Respect
- __ Service
- __ Team Work
- __ Travel
- __ Wealth

STEP TWO: Focus on the ones you put a check beside, those that fit YOU. Transfer each of those to a slip of paper or a file card.

STEP THREE: Arrange the slips of paper on a line in front of you (left to right). Pick up the first two on the left and quickly, within three seconds, decide which is most important to you. Put that slip of paper above the line, and the other slip below the line. Continue down the line until half of the slips are above and half are below. Put the slips from below in a stack to one side.

STEP FOUR: Use the same process with the slips that were above the line. Pick up the first two and quickly decide which is most important to you. Continue in the same manner until you are left with your most important value. The ones most recently below the line are your next most important values.

STEP FIVE: Sift through your discard pile to see if there are any which strongly resonate. Add them to your values stack.

Notes

Were there any surprises for you? Which values did you have the most difficulty choosing between? Are you currently living your life according to your top values?

 DIGGING A LITTLE DEEPER

Look at a recent "To Do" list or your daily planner for the past week. Compare how you spent your time with your top three values. Does the way you spent your time and your values match or is there a disconnect?

Telephone a friend or meet them for coffee to discuss what you discovered.

As you look at your next week's activities, what are ways you could emphasize or incorporate your top values?

Are you willing to commit to doing that? How will you know you've succeeded? Write down your plan.

Lay out the boundaries of your garden space on a piece of graph paper.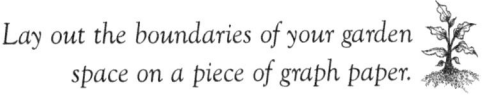

How Do You See It?
Perception Determines Action

In designing a garden space, the gardener sees where the garden space ends and another space begins. There are boundaries such as property lines and buildings as well as natural features that form the edges and contours of the garden. For human beings, the way we see the world and the words we use to describe ourselves, others, and the events of our lives form our boundaries and determine our possibilities.

There are many facts in our lives. Facts include such items as time and place of birth, our years and place(s) of schooling, the type of car we drive, and our address. Much of the rest of what we talk about reflects our opinions, judgments, and assumptions. These assumptions reveal our own conditioned way of seeing and being in the world. As humans, we tend to accept our own opinions and judgments as fact.

Given our ties to personal interpretations, it's often difficult to grasp this concept. Whether or not others agree with us, we tend to think that our views and interpretations are correct and factual. However, our assumptions are not facts, but rather our interpretations of the events of our lives and who we are. Once we understand that, we have much more power to create changes in our lives. We can then choose to reinterpret past or present events and open new possibilities for action.

Designing

In a garden, the areas tend to be clearly defined and evident to everyone who visits the garden. Events in our lives and future possibilities, however, are not clearly defined. Our understanding of them is open to a great deal of interpretation.

Use the exercise on the next page to get a greater sense of possibilities for interpretation.

The Observer's Eyes

What do you see in this picture? Look at it for a few minutes to see as many possibilities as you can.

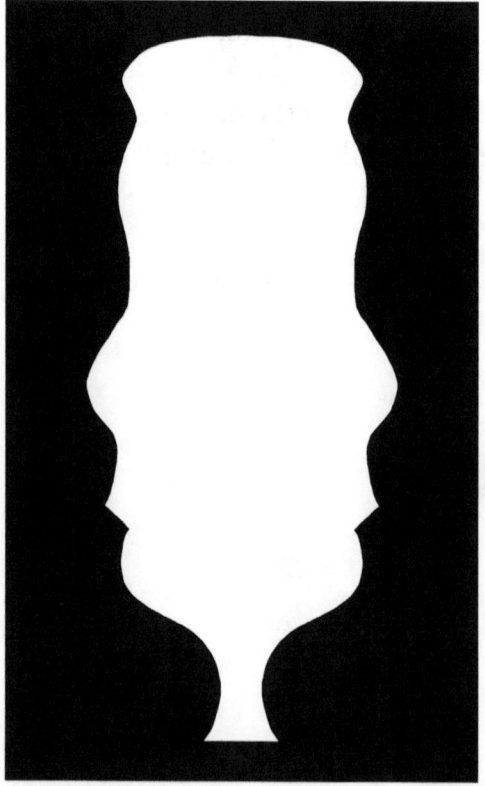

Show the picture to one or two other people and ask how many different things they can see as possibilities in this picture.

Notes

What happened? How did others see the picture? Did they see what you saw? Could you see what they saw? What possibilities did sharing interpretations open for you?

 **DIGGING A LITTLE DEEPER**

Here are some of the interpretations of other viewers: urn, two people facing away from each other, vase, cave opening, tunnel, lamp with shade, section of an ornate table leg, end view of a cable car, Christmas ornament, and lake reflection.

Just as there are many ways to interpret a picture, so there are many different ways to look at events in your life. Choose one event that has impacted the way you see the world. Write in a journal or dialogue with a friend about the event. Discover at least four other interpretations you might have made about that same event.

Which interpretation offers the greatest possibilities for moving forward in your life the way you want?

An accurate evaluation of your garden's conditions can make the difference between a garden that flourishes and one that doesn't.

What's Your Reaction Pattern?
Responding On Auto-Pilot

Just as plants are programmed to turn toward the light, we each have predictable ways of speaking and acting when something unexpected happens. The unexpected could be someone cutting us off on the freeway. Perhaps we miscalculated the amount of time a task would take or we counted on a key ingredient for dinner, only to discover it disappeared during the day. Perhaps, with no warning, our boss has just added yet another responsibility to our job or has handed us a layoff notice.

When caught off guard, each of us reacts within our own particular pattern. We might pull away and not want to deal with it. We may feel angry and want to go into immediate action to "take care of" the problem. We might draw a blank and not know what to do, or we may immediately check with others. During these times of reacting, our minds tend to run in a familiar refrain, following a well-worn script.

Certain muscles tense, and our body shapes itself into a customary structure. Our fists might clench or we might take a step back. We human beings learned reaction patterns at an early age. Survival as a species depended in part on the brain's structured fight-or-flight response. In addition, our own biochemical makeup, our early conditioning, and our interpretations about the expectations of our family, business associates, and friends have all determined our reactions to current situations.

Designing

Reaction to light is part of a plant's biological structure. Our reaction to the events in our lives is part of our human biological and psychological structure.

While our usual reactions may be appropriate in many instances, that same reaction will not serve our best interests in other situations. If we want to make changes, learning to recognize our own patterns is the first and perhaps largest step.

Do the following exercise over the next several days to notice and better understand your own personal patterns.

Fight, Flight, or Freeze

Watch yourself over the next several days when something unexpected happens. If you drive, watch your reactions in traffic. When you're standing in lines, listen to your internal conversations. Feel which muscles tense and notice your jaw. What happens when someone makes a request or gives you an order?

What do you notice about your body's reactions?

- Do you tend to 'flee' by backing away or giving up or giving in?

- Do you freeze and adopt a 'wait and see' attitude?

- Do you tense some of your muscles and get ready to fight or argue?

- Does your reaction depend on a particular situation or the people present or how you're feeling?

- Do you notice yourself leaning into or away from the person or activity?

Knowing how your body reacts and recognizing the story in your head helps you move more quickly from a reaction mode to a response mode. Reactions are automatic; response is implied choice.

Notes

If you were to characterize your usual reaction, what would it be? In situations where you are interacting with others, are your physical reactions the same when you initiate the interaction as when the other person initiates? If it tends to be a different reaction, what do you make of that?

 ### Digging a Little Deeper

As you begin to pay attention to your automatic responses, you may wonder what to do about them. The bad news is that this will always be your body's first response. The good news is that you don't have to be imprisoned by that reaction. You can now recognize your body's signals and understand that this is your way of reacting.

Once you recognize and accept your body's natural reaction, centering your body is the next step. To center, first notice where you are in the environment. Then focus on the sensations in your feet, your hands, and your head. Notice how they are placed. Feel the sensations of pressure, temperature, and tingling or streaming. Notice your breath. Sense how the air enters your mouth or nose and experience it opening your lungs and pushing your chest and abdomen forward.

Practice centering at least 10 times each day for four weeks. You might practice in your car, in your chair at work, or as you are walking down the street. Practice with the intention of feeling your body centered. Being able to center quickly allows you to choose the appropriate response in any given situation.

Designing

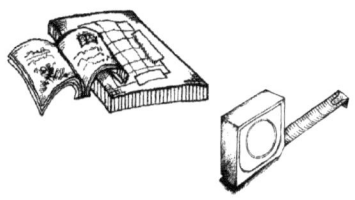

Designing a garden and a life is a great time to dream and plan, taking into account what is already present and imagining the future. In this section, you've looked at what you're satisfied with and what you value. You've recognized that your response to life reflects your interpretation of events, and you've seen that you have a natural tendency to react to events in certain ways.

This core knowledge lays the foundation for the next stage. Once you've planned, it's time to prepare the soil, begin planting, and watch as your garden and your life take shape.

SECTION TWO
PLANTING

"The first rule of successful gardening is to work with, not against, the natural setting."
Burpee Complete Gardener

Planting the Garden Outside

Once you've shaped your garden on paper, you can begin to turn your dreams into reality.

Before actually putting plants in the ground, however, you will want to prepare your soil. For most plants, the ideal garden soil is loam, a mixture of clay, silt, and sand. It has the texture of moist chocolate cake—the kind that crumbles a little when you slice it. If you're fortunate enough to have this type of soil already, hurrah! Know your soil. If it's not the right type for the plants you want, don't fret. Although soil texture cannot be changed, short of totally replacing it, it can be enhanced by incorporating a generous layer of organic material, such as farmyard manure or compost. Not only will the structure and drainage characteristics of your soil improve, but it will become more fertile, which in turn will support a lush, vibrant garden.

Next, using measuring tape, stakes, and string, mark the beds, lawns, and other planting areas according to your paper plan. Spacing may seem excessive, but your plants must be allowed the room to reach maturity. This is also the point at which irrigation lines and electrical components can be installed. It's tempting to skip over these steps now in favor of the actual planting, but laying a good foundation early on pays off down the road.

When buying plants, the gardener is faced with choices. Seeds, bulbs, and various sizes of transplants all beckon, and the good gardener knows there are advantages and disadvantages to each. Large shrubs and trees, for example, have good immediate fill-in effect, but they're more expensive and heavier to plant. Smaller plants may look scrawny by comparison but can catch up to the overall size of a larger specimen in one decent growing season. In addition, smaller plants have had less time to get used to container life and generally experience less transplant shock. Inexpensive annuals and tender perennials are a great option for brightening up and filling in a border or for creating "rivers" of color, but must be replaced every year.

Only you can decide what your time, wallet, and back will bear!

Putting your new trees, shrubs, and perennials in the ground is relatively straightforward. As the saying goes, plant them with the green side up! Generally speaking, a hole should be as deep and twice as wide as the roots of your new plant. After placing the plant in the hole, carefully tamp down the soil around the plant and water generously. Finish with a dressing of mulch, such as walk-on bark or redwood chips. Not only will this protect the plant's roots from extremes of temperature, but it will also inhibit weeds and look handsome to boot.

Other choices for your garden include seeds and bulbs. Seeds are often a good, economical choice for quick-growing plants, such as annuals, biennials, and vegetables. These plants go through their entire life—germination, blooming, setting seed, and dying—in one or two growing seasons. You can either start them indoors in starter pots, or sow them directly in place in the garden after all danger of frost has passed.

"Bulb" is the common name for a group of plants that grow from an underground structure, or a kind of specialized root. This "bulb" fuels the plant's growth and bloom, and then serves as a storage facility for nutrient reserves during its dormancy, or period of rest. The largest group of spring-flowering bulbs, which includes tulips and daffodils, are planted in the fall. A much smaller set of autumn-flowering bulbs, such as some crocuses, are planted in spring.

Follow the planting instructions that come with the bulbs. These directions tell the best planting time for your area and the ideal depth for placement. Then let nature work her magic! After resting in the soil, some bulbs even naturalize. That is, they come back year after year in greater numbers, which can be a lovely surprise in the spring.

PLANTING

Planting an outside garden requires making choices and taking time and making the effort to do the work. There is also a vast inner garden to cultivate and plant a future.

Come, enter the garden within ...

> *If your soil isn't the right type for the plants you want, don't fret.*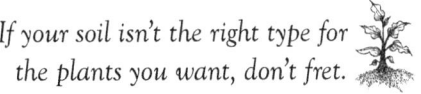

What Do You Mean, Practice?
Planting Habits

Even when a gardener carefully selects only the best seeds and cuttings for planting, the plants won't grow to their full potential without proper soil preparation and placement. The same holds true for our lives. In addition to awareness of our own personal habits of breathing, eating, drinking liquids, and other regular routines, our human soil needs regular practices as a foundation. Consciously paying attention to what and how we practice within our lives gives more energy and direction for growing the lives we want.

Think of a practice as something we do on a regular basis to train our body and mind around what we care about and value. A practice may be keeping a commitment to walk daily or visiting the gym three times a week as a way to take care of our health. The practice may be reading from a spiritual book, praying, or meditating each morning.

Or a practice may be to write five things we are grateful for in a journal each evening. A practice could be as simple as paying each bill as it comes in as a way to have a better sense of our financial picture. It might be walking our dog at a specific time each day in order to build structure into our life. A practice might even include directly facing what we are afraid of in order to increase our capacity to deal with fear.

When we are clear about who we are, who we want to be, and what we want to accomplish with our lives, intentional practices help us achieve our goals more quickly. We strengthen our commitment to personal growth by having one or more conscious regular practices.

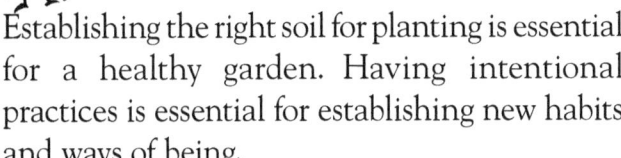

Establishing the right soil for planting is essential for a healthy garden. Having intentional practices is essential for establishing new habits and ways of being.

As you think about things you are trying to change in your life, consider your current practices. The following exercise gives you some guidelines.

Practice What You Want

Think of something you would like to accomplish within the next few months. It might be as simple as cleaning out closets or drinking more liquids. It might be as complex as becoming more patient with your children or less intimidated by your boss.

What would you like to accomplish? Write one intention here.

Now, what are you consciously doing that will help you reach that goal? For instance, if your goal is to drink more water, your practice might include filling water bottles each morning as part of your breakfast routine. It might be saying an affirmation such as, "Water feeds my body and spirit" as you walk to the car or public transportation. It might be picturing liquids flowing throughout your body, nourishing it.

Write a practice you could do daily to help you carry out the intention you wrote.

Notes

As you thought about what you want to accomplish, did you find it hard to choose just one thing? Or did you find it hard to come up with even one thing? Did you find that you have some current practices you could adapt to help you reach your goal?

 **DIGGING A LITTLE DEEPER**

One of the most important aspects in any practice is to be clear about why you are doing it. Common practices such as meditation, daily journal writing, or a daily exercise regime become much more powerful when coupled with a vocalized declaration of why you are doing the practice.

For example, suppose you walk for twenty minutes a day. What is your purpose? What do you hope to accomplish? Are you building a healthier body? Are you giving yourself time to be in nature? Are you fast-walking to build your endurance and lung capacity?

Know your purpose. In the above example, suppose you decided to walk in order to gain more appreciation of nature's beauty. As a declaration you might say at the beginning of your walk, "I am walking for the sake of feeding my spirit with the beauty in nature." Beginning each daily walk in this way, you will find that gradually you are seeing more and more of nature's beauty and feeling your spirit becoming more refreshed on your walks.

Laying a good foundation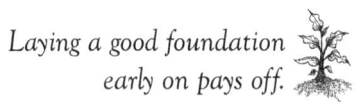
early on pays off.

Whom Do You Trust?
Sustaining Relationships

Lack of care in soil preparation or ignoring planting instructions can inhibit a plant's potential and may even cause the plant to die. In the same way, lack of trust can endanger or kill human communication and relationships. Relationships are planted in the soil of trust. As humans, we need to be able to trust that when people say something, they mean it. We need to trust that when someone tells us they'll do something, they will.

Building and maintaining trust is an ongoing challenge for organizations, groups, and individuals. When someone requests that we do something and we agree and say we'll do it, in the other person's mind, we've already completed that task. Even if the time for completion is in the future, the other person bases current and future actions on our fulfillment of the promise.

Sometimes we say we'll do something because we sincerely intend to do it. We also know we have the competence to do it. However, there are other times when we say we'll do something just to stall. We don't really intend to do it and we hope the other person will forget. There are also times when we say we'll do something, even though we know we lack the competence or necessary time to fulfill our promise. Yet, each time we don't keep our promises to ourselves or to others, for whatever reason, the relationship of trust breaks down. Once lack of trust begins, it becomes increasingly difficult to continue growing that relationship.

PLANTING

Just as appropriate soil and proper planting are cornerstones of a thriving garden, trust is a key ingredient for building and maintaining relationships. The next exercise invites you to explore your personal definitions of trust.

Trustworthy People

Make a list of people you trust. If you trust yourself, add your name to the list. Beside each person's name, write why you are judging him or her to be trustworthy.

Name	Trustworthy Qualities

Notes

What did you notice as you thought about people you consider trustworthy? Did you include yourself? Did you find that trust is situational? How did a person's ability to keep agreements and promises affect your assessment of them as trustworthy?

 DIGGING A LITTLE DEEPER

What happens when the soil of trust breaks down? What can you do to maintain or rebuild yourself as a trustworthy person? In looking back over your list of trustworthy qualities, is the ability to keep promises part of that list?

One of the most common challenges today is finding or making time to meet the commitments and keep the promises we make. On a sheet of paper, write some of the promises you've made within the past week. Include promises to people at work, to family members, to friends, and to yourself.

Now, look at your list and answer the following questions:

- Is there really enough time to keep those promises?
- Are the promises equally important?
- Who will suffer most if you don't keep the promise?
- Did you fully intend to keep each promise?

If you recognize that you will be unable to keep a promise, renegotiate with the person and agree to a new timeline or promise.

PLANTING

> *Your plants must be allowed the room to reach maturity.*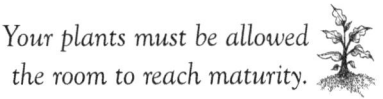

What Are You Nipping in the Bud?
Timing Is Critical

Timing is critical in gardening. Seeds, young plants, and bulbs or cuttings need to be planted after the danger of frost has passed. Water and nourishment need to come at the right time in the growing cycle. There are also times when plants need to be left alone to grow in their own time. After all, you can't keep digging up a bulb to make sure it's growing!

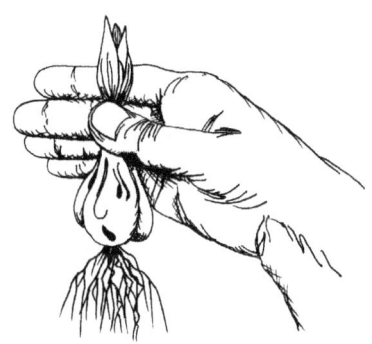

As human beings, we get seeds of ideas about how things might be different. We get our idea seeds about new ways of being, doing, and having. When we're fully focused, we can often see in our mind's eye and feel 'in our bones' a whole cycle of change. In fact, we sometimes get so many ideas and see so many possibilities, that it's difficult to choose which ideas to nurture and grow.

To grow ideas to maturity, we must provide an incubation time so they don't burst forth prematurely. Ideas and plans need time to gather enough energy to grow fully. Many of us are like the impatient gardener who wants to keep digging in the soil to check on plant growth. What we really need is to cultivate patience and allow the sensations of anticipation to build.

Both seeds and ideas need the right conditions in which to grow. Just as proper soil preparation is essential for successful gardening, it's also important to build enough energy and support to grow plans and ideas to maturity. The first step to increase your ability to build your foundation is to recognize the body sensations of impatience.

The following exercise is designed to help you identify some of those physical sensations. Recognizing the sensations, without acting on them, helps you build your capacity to implement plans and ideas.

Temptation

At a time when you're hungry, put a favorite food on a plate in front of you. Place the plate so that it's near enough to touch, but don't reach out for the food. Notice your body sensations. Notice what you do with your eyes and with your jaw and with your mouth. Notice which body muscles you tense. Listen to what is running through your mind. Notice if and how you distract yourself from the food.

Let your desire to eat the food build. Savor the energy of that desire rather than yielding to it.

Notes

Where in your body did you notice an urge to eat? Did you have any tendency to reach for the food? Did you speak to yourself as you were doing the exercise? Did you stay focused on the food or did you distract yourself? If you distracted yourself, how did you do that?

Digging a Little Deeper

In the Temptation exercise, what did you notice? Learning to tolerate the sensations that come with impatience for action is an important life skill. Becoming more aware of your own body sensations as you go about regular work will give you further clues that will help you change patterns.

During the next week, notice when you jump from task to task. Instead of getting distracted by e-mail, the refrigerator, or shuffling papers, try sitting for 10-20 seconds and just notice what is happening in your body.

- Which muscles are you tensing?
- Which muscles are you relaxing?
- Do you feel heat or cold in any part of your body? Which part(s)?
- What thoughts are going through your mind?
- What do you notice about your jaw and your facial muscles in general?

The exercise outlined above will help you further identify body signals which accompany your restless behavior. Once you have identified the sensation, you are in a better place to choose staying with what you are doing or jumping to the new thing. Knowing your own signals means you won't be held a prisoner of impatience.

Know your soil.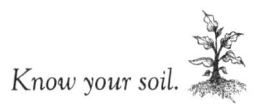

What Mood?
Tilling Your Emotional Soil

A gardener knows the soil needs of each specific plant. Although some soils require much preparation and adjustment so the plants can grow to be healthy and strong, others need little work. Recognizing our own "soil" of predominant moods and emotions as well as knowing ways to shift them helps us as we grow and change throughout our lives.

Events in our lives trigger emotional reactions. Our emotions are constantly shifting according to what's happening around us and how we interpret those events. Some of the time we consciously recognize our emotions and at other times, our emotions pass beneath our level of conscious thought.

Moods, on the other hand, last longer. We each have our own set of predominant moods we tend to fall into. Each mood shapes our body in certain ways, determines what we see as possibilities for action, and creates or replays a story that runs through our head.

For instance, in a mood of hopefulness, we can see numerous possibilities for solving a particular problem and we feel energized to try one or more of those possibilities. Our posture is upright and our story is one of, "I can do this." In a mood of resignation, however, we don't see much hope for things getting better, nor do we have the energy to try. Our posture slumps, and the words running through our mind reflect our 'what's the use' mood.

PLANTING

A soil's consistency and nutrients help determine what plants you can grow. Moods and emotions live in your body and help determine what you think is possible. Recognizing your own emotional soil opens the way for potential new actions. The list on the following page helps you identify your most typical emotional spaces.

Think about your usual moods and emotions. What words come to mind? Are you usually optimistic or pessimistic? When things don't go your way, what is your tendency? Do you fall into a resigned mood, become filled with resentment, or do you look at those situations as a challenge?

Read the list on the following page and highlight those emotions you identify with most strongly.

In the Mood

Accepting	Accomplished	Adventurous
Afraid	Angry	Annoyed
Anxious	Apprehensive	Arrogant
Blue	Challenged	Comfortable
Compassionate	Competitive	Confident
Connected	Contented	Controlled
Creative	Curious	Determined
Dejected	Delighted	Disgusted
Disdainful	Embarrassed	Enjoying
Envious	Excited	Fearful
Focused	Friendly	Frustrated
Grateful	Guilty	Healthy
Humble	Indignant	Independent
Irritated	Jealous	Joyful
Justified	Kindly	Loving
Loyal	Miserable	Neutral
Nostalgic	Nurturing	Obliged
Open	Optimistic	Parental
Passionate	Peaceful	Perplexed
Pessimistic	Pitying	Playful
Pleased	Powerful	Prideful
Productive	Purposeful	Quiet
Regretful	Resentful	Resigned
Resolute	Respectful	Responsible
Sad	Scared	Secure
Serene	Shame	Smug
Stable	Successful	Surprised
Tolerant	Trusting	Upset
Unhappy	Worried	Zestful

Notes

What did you notice as you read through the list? Were there some words on the list that stood out for you? Did you notice yourself thinking that it depends on the situation? For instance, you may associate certain moods with work situations and a different set of moods with family or particular groups of friends.

 ### Digging a Little Deeper

Since emotions often involve physiological changes, they help determine what you think is possible in a given situation. Notice what happens when you try the following:

Put your body in a sad position by drooping your shoulders and hanging your head. Now say, "I am REALLY happy!" three times. What happened? How did your voice sound?

Now straighten up. Put your shoulders back and raise your head. Smile broadly and say three times, "I am SO sad." What happened?

You learned your predominant moods early in life and you fall into them automatically. However, once you recognize your own natural tendency toward particular dispositions, you can choose whether you want to stay there or shift to a different one. When you want to change moods, you can modify your body position, alter your facial expression, move to a different area of the room, or focus your eyes on another space in your environment. Listening to music is yet another way to vary your disposition. Changing moods then becomes a conscious decision.

PLANTING

Planting a garden and living a life require making decisions and expending effort. In planting for your future, you need to establish practices that will help you achieve your goals. In this section you looked at issues of trust, recognized that many of your ideas and plans need time to incubate, and examined your personal mood soil.

Once you've planted, you will need to continue tending your life to achieve the maximum potential for growth.

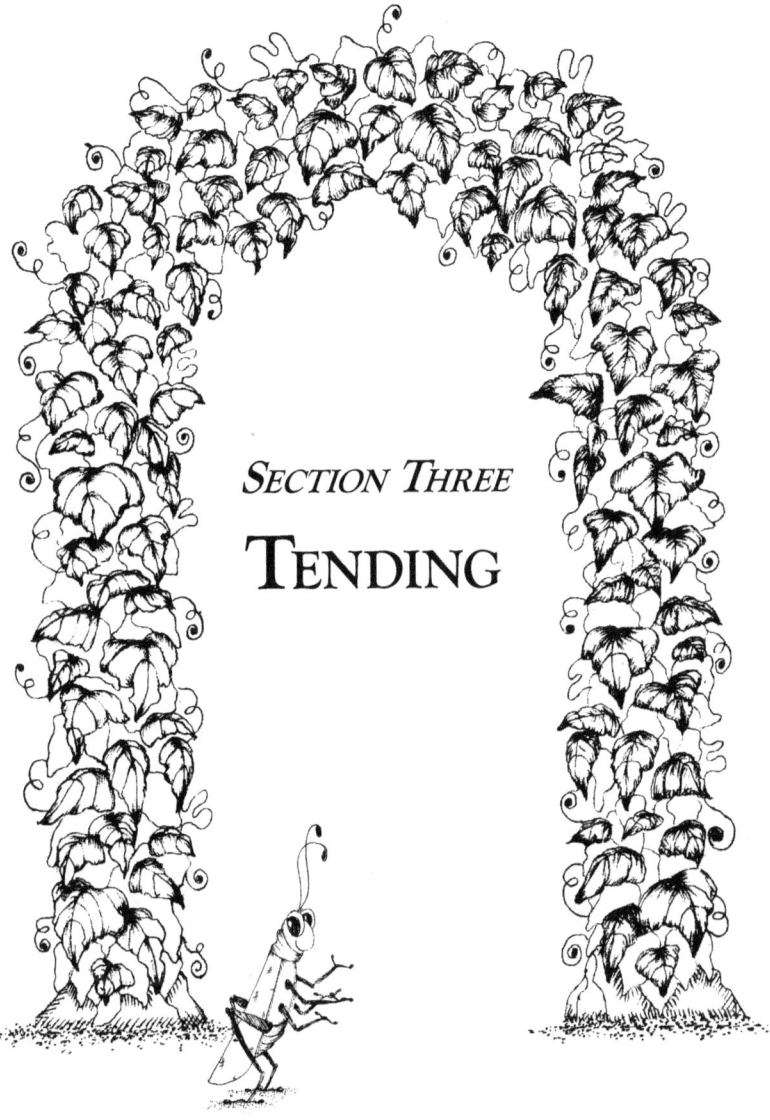

Section Three
Tending

"Once you understand what makes plants tick, you'll understand what you need to do to help them grow."
Barbara Damrosch

Tending the Garden Outside

Designing and planting are only the beginnings of a successful garden. No matter what kind of a garden you have, or what stage of life it's in, you'll need routines to keep it growing. The good news is there's no mystique to good gardening; you just have to think like a plant!

A plant's needs and wants are simple. It needs water when it's thirsty and food when it is low on nutrients. It needs shelter from harsh weather such as sudden extremes of temperature, sun, rain, or wind. It needs room to spread its roots and branches without competition from other plants, and it needs protection from insects, birds, and animals. It also wants regular grooming, such as deadheading or pruning, to encourage new growth.

Like people, though, no two plants are alike in exactly how they want their general needs met. Once you understand your plants, and know each one's natural habits and specific preferences, you can nurture them appropriately.

When plants like their environment and are well-tended, they reward you with handsome looks and vitality. Sometimes, however, we don't heed the signs of need. We miss the pest that's destroying a plant's foliage, or we underestimate a shrub's mature size. Perhaps we're caught by an unexpected frost. And so some of our plants languish. Some, let's face it, expire. But it's often from these mistakes—and there will be mistakes—that we learn the most about our garden, more even than from our successes.

For gardening is a continual learning process. Key in this process is the concept of balanced care. A massive, frenzied once-a-season cleanup is one way to tend your garden. However, it is not a very effective way of maintaining beauty and vitality—yours or the garden's!

The first step in giving balanced care is to gain familiarity with your garden. Check your plants regularly, and learn what's "normal" for your plants.

While you're checking your plants, also take the opportunity to pick off spent blossoms, clip wilted stalks, and dig out weeds. Keeping your garden cleaned up in this way can minimize pest and disease problems.

The second step of the learning process is to understand the significance of an unhealthy-looking plant. Some symptoms are no more than nuisances, while others may indicate the presence of a more serious disease that you will want to keep from spreading to your healthy plants. Until you know the difference between nuisance and serious problem, your local nursery can help determine the extent of the challenge.

Next, you need to know when to act, and when to wait the problem out. With our fast-paced lives, we tend to value action and rapid problem-solving. In gardening, however, sometimes it pays to be patient. Not all insect infestations require chemical solutions, and not all insects are pests.

Ladybugs and lacewing larvae, for example, reach maturity in the spring approximately three weeks after aphids, and a ladybug's idea of a delectable feast is a nice, juicy aphid.

Even with real, certified pests, you can often implement natural solutions. You're probably not a gardener who welcomes snails into your garden. Before reaching for the snail bait, however, consider that ducks just love snails. And a duck happily provides you with an endless supply of fertilizer! Smart gardeners encourage beneficial insects and animals to make the garden their home by selecting the plants that naturally attract them.

In the meantime, young pests (and here I'm talking about harmful insects, not the neighbor children) can be deterred with a strong jet of water from your garden hose or by handpicking. Just remember that a truly pest-free garden does not exist.

TENDING

Lush garden growth requires on-going awareness and consistent garden care and maintenance. So, too, our garden of the self needs tending.

        Come, enter the garden within ...

A plant's needs and wants are simple.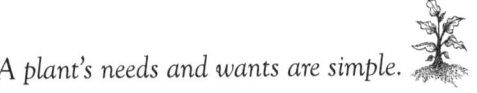

Taking Care of Basics?
Breathing and Other Necessities

A gardener must take care of the basics or soon there'll be no garden. Every gardener needs to water, weed, prune plants, fertilize the soil, and take care of pests in order to have a flourishing garden. Plants will show when they are not taken care of. They wither, they don't have healthy color, and they don't develop as they should when they are not properly cared for.

As people, we also need regular care and feeding or we cannot act effectively in life. We don't have energy for doing what we want to do and our bodies may have less resistance to disease. Taking care of basics means getting enough sleep, drinking enough liquids, and eating foods that nourish rather than deplete or go straight to fat storage. Knowing how to move to deep, centered breathing when we are anxious or afraid is also a way to take care of some of the fundamentals of life.

TENDING

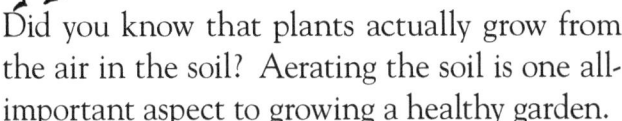

Did you know that plants actually grow from the air in the soil? Aerating the soil is one all-important aspect to growing a healthy garden.

As a human being, you probably tend not to think about your breathing. You've been breathing automatically from the time you were born. Yet when you are afraid or in a stressful situation, you tend to breathe shallowly and even stop breathing for a bit. Notice what happens when you do this next exercise.

Just Breathe

Breathing is essential for detoxifying your body, energizing you, and regulating organs and tissues in your body. Proper breathing strengthens your immune system and transforms the way you sense and feel about yourself.

As you are reading these words, silently or aloud, notice where your breath is. Is it shallow and high in your chest? Where do you pause — at the end of your inhale or at the end of your exhale or somewhere in the middle? Do you usually breathe through your nose or your mouth? Can you consciously change the rate and placement of your breath?

Knowing how to breathe consciously enables you to pause and regroup when life becomes hectic. This capacity to pause and breathe gives you great power to move in the world. Just lifting your shoulders doesn't do it. Breathing deeply expands your abdomen and opens your chest and back. Pausing to consciously breathe can change your mood.

Pick a day and remind yourself throughout that day to breathe! Put sticky reminder notes on your refrigerator, mirror, steering wheel, and computer screen.

NOTES

What did you notice about your mood and energy level after you took a few deep breaths? How difficult was it to remember to breathe? Have you caught yourself not breathing at times? What were the circumstances?

 DIGGING A LITTLE DEEPER

Research studies indicate that you get the equivalent of four cups of water from your food and one cup from metabolism. The remaining water comes from fluid intake. How much additional fluid you need depends largely on your level of activity and the climate in which you live.

Becoming an observer of your own personal self-care patterns is essential if you are interested in becoming more effective. Besides breathing, being vigilant about food and water intakes is necessary.

Keep a food diary for five consecutive days. Note not only what you eat and drink, but also how much and when. Also check your mood and energy level during the hours after you have eaten. What do you notice?

No matter what kind of garden you have,
you'll need some routines to keep it going.

Routine? What Routine?
CULTIVATING USEFUL SYSTEMS

Garden design plans need to consider not only how a garden will eventually look, but also how it can be maintained. Part of a complete design includes pathways for moving about in the space as well as systems and schedules for watering, nourishing, pruning, and replanting.

As in a garden, our lives need balanced care rather than extremes. In your own life design, you probably have routines you follow. For instance, you most likely have a regular sequence for getting ready for the day, as well as regular wake-up and go-to-bed times. How about regular times for eating or exercise?

For instance, some of us regularly have to go on a car key hunt while other folks have a particular place where they always put their keys. In a grocery store, some people wander through the aisles looking for various products while others have a routine for meal planning and shopping.

Successful gardeners have regular daily or weekly schedules for watering plants. They fertilize the soil, weed particular areas, and deadhead and prune plants on a fairly regular schedule. Less successful gardeners do the necessary work of maintaining a garden only when the spirit moves them.

To some people, having routines sounds boring and less than spontaneous. However, those folks who have a number of daily routines in place have freed themselves from constantly having to make decisions about those things they must do anyway. That, in turn, frees their energy for more creative pursuits.

Gardeners need to follow some routines to keep their plants healthy and growing. The following exercise gives you an opportunity to recognize your personal routines and consider areas where a routine – or a different routine – might help smooth some current rough patches.

Think of what you do in each of the following areas and make notes for each section. If you have no set routine in that section, consider how that lack might be impacting your life and your current stress levels.

The questions in this section cover only a small portion of your possible daily routines. Use more paper to list others you already have in place. If you have a family, you may prefer to look at these questions in terms of them as well as yourself.

It's Automatic

What is your sequence of activities as you get ready for a workday?

What is your sequence of activities as you get ready for bed?

Do you have specific times for getting up and going to bed?

Do you have specific times of the day for meals?

What is your exercise schedule?

What is your maintenance routine for home cleaning and picking up?

How do you usually take care of your daily mail, e-mail, and phone messages at work and at home?

How do you usually take care of bill paying and your accounts? Do you pay them as they come in, on a certain day of the week or month, or when you remember to do so?

NOTES

As you read through the list of potential areas for routines, what did you notice? Do you have some routines so embedded that you don't even realize they are routines? How well are your current routines working for you?

 ### Digging a Little Deeper

Having routines in place releases energy for other pursuits. As you thought over your current routines, you may have noticed some are firmly in place and working very well. Hurrah!

However, you may be lacking some routines or there may be some that need adjusting to help you function more effectively. Decide on one routine you'd like to incorporate or fine tune.

What is it?

Where will you fit it into your schedule?

How will you know if it's working?

Now practice your chosen routine for AT LEAST 21 days.

A plant wants regular grooming, such as dead-heading or pruning, to encourage new growth.

Is It Time to Let Go?
Weeding Your Relationship Garden

In order for gardens to bloom and grow, gardeners need to keep weeding. Weeding takes effort, and it's easy to overlook or put off this task because other things seem ever so much more interesting.

In the same way, it is very easy to let things and habits accumulate long after they've served their purpose in our lives. They may have been useful at one time but they no longer serve us. And there they sit, taking our space and our physical and emotional energy!

These things and habits are relics from our past. They keep distracting us from what's really important in our lives now as we are building our future. When we know exactly what we value and care about, it is much easier to weed out what no longer belongs.

There are groups and organizations we belong to, as well as people we interact with, who were important at one time in our life. Depending on our current goals and life stage, some may no longer be important to us. Making periodic efforts to look at how we spend our time and who we spend it with is an important activity.

Weeding is an essential gardening activity. The following exercise allows you to begin your own weeding process.

Begin your weeding by noticing who you spend your time with during a typical week. If you keep a day planner, last week's plan may serve as a reminder. If you don't keep a planner, you might jot down who you spent time with during the day on index cards or in a journal. The best time to do this may be at bedtime. Use that information to complete the following exercise.

People and Time

If you looked at your non-sleep time as 100% during a typical week, what percent of your time do you spend with each of the following? Although some categories may have a zero because they don't fit you, the total should add up to 100%.

___ Your children

___ Your co-workers/colleagues

___ Your spouse/significant other

___ Your clients/customers

___ Your parents/family members

___ People you don't know

___ Friends

___ Yourself

___ Acquaintances/neighbors

___ Other

___ Total

Notes

What do you notice? How are you making your decisions about using your time? Which things, habits, and groups of people give you the most satisfaction? Which are the most frustrating? As you look at your time allocations, is that what you want? Do you have any weeding to do?

 DIGGING A LITTLE DEEPER

Think about the people you currently spend much of your time with. Do they nourish you and help you grow, or do they pull on your energy and leave you feeling drained?

Are there ways you might spend less time with those who drain and more time with those who nourish? Sometimes it's fairly easy. Relationships with acquaintances and co-workers provide flexibility. For instance, you can determine with whom you'll sit at a meeting or whether you'll have coffee with a certain group of people.

Family members and clients who drain you present a stronger challenge. Assuming you want or need to continue these relationships, the following questions will be useful in developing a strategy for your weeding process:

- Are there particular times when you feel more drained when you are around these people?
- Are there any times you could include uplifting people when meeting with these folks?
- Can you send energy from your heart to theirs while you are with them?
- Can you creatively find humor in the situation?

Write out a strategy you will try in order to get more nourishment from your relationships.

Gardening is a continual learning process. The first step is to gain familiarity with your garden.

Do You Hear That Voice?
Training Your Inner Critic

To get the best results, many gardeners talk to their plants. Talking to plants is one thing; much more important is what we say to ourselves.

We all have a constant voice speaking inside our head. It may be a narrator, telling us what we're doing and what's going on around us. Sometimes the voice is that of our parents or friends, or even our children. We may have a motivating voice or a judging voice. Our inner voice may vary with circumstances and our current mood.

Each of us interprets our world through eyes shaped by early experiences and relationships. The cultures into which we were born and in which we currently live continue to impact our interpretations of events in our lives and actions of others. In addition, our self-concept is often created based on our understanding of others' opinions about us. Those interpretations, through our inner voice, tell us what we believe to be true.

Many gardeners speak lovingly to their plants. It is interesting to ask yourself what kind of an inner voice you use. Is your voice usually planning your next moves? Is it judging you and others harshly? Is your inner voice often a cheerleader? What kinds of inner conversations do you hold?

Use the exercise on the next page to become more aware of the power of your inner voice.

All Ears

Begin noticing what kinds of language you are using with yourself. Imagine you are an outsider listening to your inner voice for a period of time. Take notes about what you notice.

- Did you encourage yourself to try something you thought of as a challenge?

- Did you criticize something you had done or not done?

- Did you spend a lot of time worrying about what other people were thinking?

- Did you remind yourself to keep on track with what you wanted to accomplish?

- If you were to guess, what percentage of time were you:

	_____ planning?
	_____ criticizing yourself?
	_____ criticizing others?
	_____ imagining conversations?
	_____ cheering yourself?
	_____ other? _____

NOTES

What did you notice about your inner voice? Were there any surprises when you consciously paid attention to how you talk to yourself? What patterns did you hear? Were there some things you noticed that you'd like to change?

 **Digging a Little Deeper**

Noticing how your inner voice sounds and when and how you listen to it are steps in exercising choice over the direction of your life.

Suppose you discovered (or verified) that your voice is highly critical much of the time? What would you like to do about what you discovered? One way to begin breaking a pattern is to interrupt it. Try one of the following as pattern interrupters, or develop a pattern interrupter of your own.

- Be a comedian and ask your voice, just for the day, to comment on your life as a comedian would. See how many ways you can find to laugh about things you normally pass judgment on or criticize.

- Be a cheerleader of yourself for one day. Make up a short cheer and say it to yourself whenever you notice your critical voice rising to the surface. Encourage yourself. Cheer yourself on to achieve, to endure, or whatever is called for at the time.

- Imagine your inner voice is a radio. Turn down the volume when you notice criticism.

TENDING

Tending a garden and a life is a process. In this section, you reminded yourself of basic self-care, looked at the importance of routines to free your energy for achieving your goals, began weeding what no longer belonged, and listened to your inner voice to consider whether it was creating an impetus or an obstacle to your dreams.

Now it's time to focus on enjoying the fruits of your labor.

SECTION FOUR

ENJOYING

"...who has planted a garden feels that he has done something for the good of the whole world."
Charles Dudley Warner

Enjoying the Garden Outside

The process is complete. You've imagined a garden that suits both your personality and the character of the space it fills. You've brought it into reality by planning, preparing, planting, and pampering. Your garden is flourishing, sometimes in ways you expected, other times surprising you. And you've begun the whole cycle again.

In the designing, planting, and tending stages of the garden process, the focus was on the work of growing and maintaining a garden. Along with the tasks, however, are a myriad of ways to enjoy the garden during every phase of the garden cycle.

The garden, like all of life, operates in a cycle of birth, growth, reproduction, and decline. Seeds begin to send roots down into the soil and sprout leaflets. The seedlings grow, devoting their early energy to the development of leaves, stems, and branches. Depending on type and growth habits, plants may take a season or many years to reach maturity. Along the way, they blossom and set fruit, and in that process, produce seeds, spores, or tubers for the next generation. They may take periods of rest, or dormancy, to accumulate stores of energy to see them through another cycle of growth, blossoming, and fruiting. And at the end of their life cycle, they die back as their life energy wanes.

The amazing thing is, at any point in time, different parts of your garden are at different stages of life. Each stage offers sights, sounds, and scents to lift your spirits. Thus the garden offers an on-going source of satisfaction. No matter what type of garden you have, or what season it is, your garden is a feast for the senses.

Take pleasure in the cool, earthy feel of damp soil as you plant a seedling. Indulge in the heady scent of ripe raspberries or tomatoes. Let yourself be captured by the crackle of fallen leaves under your feet, or by the sight of a spider web on a bare tree, glistening in the morning dew.

Enjoy also the play of color and texture, light and shadow. There is the whisper of a breeze through foliage, the steady hum of bees, the crunch of gravel underfoot. You may catch the sound of tiny, trilling sparrows as they build a nest in your hanging begonia, or smell the fresh green scent of a newly mown lawn. The soft furriness of lamb's ears leaves, the prick of fir needles, and the soft velvet of a rose petal are there to enjoy at other times. In fact, there is always something wonderful tempting your senses in the garden, if you take the time to appreciate it.

Have you ever admired, perhaps with a twinge of envy, a special garden in the neighborhood? That yard is the one that always looks so luxuriant, so full, and so vital. It doesn't look like that gardener ever experiences 'mistakes' in gardening! At times, you may despair of your garden ever achieving such glorious heights. But remember those veteran gardeners may have been gardening for fifty-odd years. They have lived the cycle many times over, and know that the garden keeps growing, year after year, ever changing. They have learned what works in their yards and how to coax plants along.

With that in mind, you can limit that envious green to your thumbs, and see in her garden not only the potential yours holds, but the opportunities for celebration it offers. Feast on the sight of a perfect pink rosebud or a monarch butterfly flitting among the bottlebrush shrubs. Or cheer the completion of a weeding cycle. The important thing is to take time to appreciate what's right in the garden in this moment, not just what needs watering, or pruning, or weeding.

For a garden lets you enjoy the moment. You don't need to think about what could have been, or what might be tomorrow. In a garden, you can live in the here and now.

ENJOYING

The visible space of the garden outside provides many ways to enjoy the process and results of gardening. We can also increase enjoyment in all aspects of our lives when we look inside.

Come, enter the garden within…

Your garden is a feast for the senses.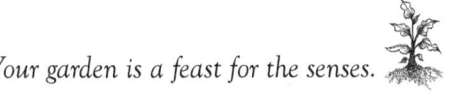

What's Worth Celebrating?
FUELING YOUR ENTHUSIASM

There is much to celebrate in a garden. Taking time to acknowledge the completion of a planting or weeding cycle or to appreciate the scent of a special flower gives meaning to a gardener's efforts.

Normally, celebrations recognize major accomplishments, or the beginnings or endings of a phase of life.

Celebrations usually include feasting and ritual. These may require preparation and hard work on the part of organizers and participants. However, who says celebrations need to be formal? What would happen if we looked at mini-celebrations as an important part of each day?

Most of the time, we rush from one task to another and rarely stop to enjoy the fruits of our labor or luck. How might our lives be different if we paused and celebrated in small ways? One children's book* tells the story of a girl who chooses her own celebrations, instead of limiting herself to recognized holidays. She knows what to celebrate because she notices what feeds her mind, body, and heart, and takes time to appreciate it. She pauses to gaze at a rainbow and a special cloud formation. She watches for the return of birds from their winter home and for the blooms of her favorite cactus as her signal to celebrate a new year.

For us, mini-celebrations might include smiling to ourselves in delight, sending a high-five signal to a friend, planning a special meal, or breathing down to our toes. Imagine how energizing it would be to enjoy the uplift of celebrating on a daily basis.

* *I'm In Charge of Celebrations* by Byrd Baylor

Because it requires effort to maintain a garden year after year, the gardener needs to feel enjoyment in both the process and the results of gardening.

In the same way, putting a little celebration into your everyday activities will fuel your enthusiasm and motivate you to keep going. This is especially true when your activities involve things that are unpleasant or challenging. The next exercise will give you a chance to look at opportunities to include more celebrations in your days.

Small Celebrations

If you think of a celebration as needing invitations, special foods, and the appropriate clothing, you might steer clear of organizing one because of the work involved. Look at the list below and check off how frequently you do each of these potential mini-celebrations:

Activity	Frequently	Seldom	Never
Contacting a friend to share what you've accomplished	☐	☐	☐
Having people to your home for an informal meal	☐	☐	☐
Picking or buying fresh flowers	☐	☐	☐
Sending a card to someone	☐	☐	☐
Listening to your favorite music	☐	☐	☐
Watching a sunrise or sunset	☐	☐	☐
Sitting quietly while sipping a special hot or cold drink	☐	☐	☐
Marking a completed step on a multi-step task in your day planner	☐	☐	☐
Humming or singing	☐	☐	☐
Admiring your favorite color	☐	☐	☐
Patting yourself on the back	☐	☐	☐

What other ways can you think of to acknowledge small victories during the day?

NOTES

What did you notice as you did this exercise? In which column are most of your checks? Did looking at this list remind you of some of the ways you do celebrate? What are they?

 **DIGGING A LITTLE DEEPER**

Feasting is a part of many celebrations. Eating special foods in the company of family and friends can replenish your spirits as well as your energy.

As a practice, try feasting on sights and sounds during a day. Some possible sights include the colors in a prism, a dog's eyes, or a great double play during a baseball game. Sounds could include the hum of a crowd, the voice of a loved one, or the sound of running water.

List here at least ten sights and sounds you will feast on tomorrow:

1.
2.
3.
4.
5.
6.
7.
8.
9.
10.
Others ...

Your garden is flourishing, sometimes in ways you expected, other times surprising you.

What Shows on Your Face?
Revealing Your Emotional Landscape

A garden, full of color and scent, frequently brings a smile to our face and fills us with contentment and pleasure. Recognized or not, moods, emotions, and feelings continually flow through us. Their presence can be seen in both the voluntary and involuntary muscles on the face.

Decades of research have shown that our facial expressions and our emotional moods match. Scientists can measure the physiological indicators, such as heart rate and body temperature, of various emotions such as anger, sadness, and fear. These indicators appear whether the individual is unconsciously reacting to an event or consciously changing their facial muscles.

Moods and emotions tend to determine how a person sees the world and possibilities for action. Since our face conveys to others how we are feeling, others respond based on what they notice and how they interpret our facial expression. Angry looks frequently cause others to retreat from us, while smiles often invite a smile back and provide uplifted spirits.

ENJOYING

Gardeners experience a variety of emotions while working in their gardens. They may feel delight, curiosity, satisfaction, or frustration and those emotions show in their faces.

This next exercise will increase your perceptions about facial expressions and help you become more aware of the connection between your facial expressions and emotions.

Watch That Face

This activity requires that you watch television with the sound off. Words would distract you from the purpose of this exercise.

Choose a program that shows people's faces while they are talking. Interviews, soap operas, Senate hearings, and newsmaker programs are good choices.

What do you notice about people's faces? What do you see around the muscles of their eyes and mouths? What do you think they are feeling as they speak? How do you think they want you to react?

If you can tape a few television programs, then rerun the tapes at a slower speed, you will be able to see even more shifts and changes in people's facial expressions.

Enjoying

Notes

What did you notice? Was there much change in their facial expression? Did the speakers strike you as being genuine in what they were saying? Based on what you observed, what do you think was their level of enjoyment?

 **DIGGING A LITTLE DEEPER**

Standing or sitting in front of your mirror, use some of your typical facial expressions as you imagine the following:

- Your 'to do' list
- A dent in the car
- 30 non-stop minutes of typing
- A friend greeting you
- A driver who cuts you off in traffic

As you practice different looks, keep your facial muscles in each position and notice what happens in your body. Do some muscles contract while others relax? Do you find that some looks increase your energy or motivation? Do you feel calmer with some facial expressions? How does your emotion match what you see in the mirror?

What is your look of enjoyment? What do your facial muscles do when you are enjoying an activity? Use that look the next time you want to increase your own enjoyment.

The garden offers an on-going source of satisfaction.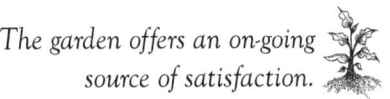

How Do You Define Success?
Conditions of Satisfaction

In order to grow to its maximum beauty and productivity, each plant needs its own unique blend of soil, space, nourishment, and water. Knowing these requirements ahead of time enables the gardener to provide the best possible conditions for each plant.

Although as human beings we can't always provide optimal conditions for our own happiness, it does help to know our own conditions of success for various activities. Conditions of success answer the question, "What will it take for me to feel this project is completed successfully?" Being able to identify and describe our criteria for satisfaction before an event or transaction takes place helps us keep focused on what is truly important about each activity. The only catch is that those conditions of satisfaction must be within our control.

Most of us decide after something is finished whether it satisfies us or not. This habit of deciding after the fact often leads to feeling dissatisfied. Because we haven't thought out what it would take for us to feel satisfied before we start, we often end up with a feeling of emptiness or a vague sense of wondering if things should be different. Knowing expectations before we begin provides more opportunities to celebrate completions.

Deciding beforehand about what you are looking for in your gardening experience helps you keep focused on the aspects most important to you. For some, it may be the physical activity involved, for others the most important aspect is the finished look of the garden.

The following activity will give you a chance to practice thinking ahead about your conditions of success for a particular activity.

CONDITIONS OF SUCCESS

Think about your next meal. At the end of the meal, how will you know if you're satisfied? The questions below will help you generate your criteria for satisfaction.

- Does there need to be a particular nutritional content?

- Do you need to feel full?

- Do you need to have energy three hours after you've eaten?

- Are a certain number of calories necessary or do certain foods need to be in the meal?

- Does the meal need to be prepared within a certain time frame?

- Do there need to be certain spices or textures in the food?

Plan and eat your meal with your specific conditions of success in mind.

Notes

Did your meal meet your conditions of success? In what ways did thinking about those conditions of satisfaction beforehand impact the experience of eating the meal? How can you use the strategy of planning conditions of satisfaction in other areas of your life?

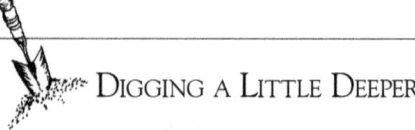 ### Digging a Little Deeper

Being able to declare that you are satisfied with someone's work or performance is a key component in human relationships. Clarity about expectations enables you to declare satisfaction at work and in personal relationships. Also, when you declare satisfaction, you provide completion for one phase of a project, and cleanly open the way for a new phase.

Think of a person you'll be interacting with tomorrow or the next day. What do you expect and want to accomplish? In order for you to feel satisfied at the end of the interaction, what will need to happen?

Keep your conditions of satisfaction in mind as you interact and notice what happens. Did thinking out beforehand what was important about this interaction impact your actions during your time together? Did you know or ask about the other person's expectations? How did you feel as you ended the interaction? Did you feel a sense of completion?

> *There is always something wonderful*
> *tempting your senses in the garden,*
> *if you take the time to appreciate it.*

How Often Do You Pause To Refresh?
Gratitude Fertilizes

Within a garden there are many reasons to feel gratitude. Sun-drenched flowers, new life, tasty herbs and vegetables, and bird songs all give reasons to appreciate and savor the gifts a garden brings.

Interestingly enough, pausing to appreciate and taking the time to express gratitude actually increase contentment and satisfaction with life in general. Expressing gratitude amplifies our good memories and allows us to experience more positive thoughts long after our initial statement of thanks. Being able to express gratitude is an emotional strength that allows us to reach beyond ourselves and connect with something larger and more permanent.

Being aware of the good things that happen to us and, more importantly, taking the time to express thanks become habits if we practice them daily. Expressing gratitude pulls our attention toward what we appreciate. It changes the way we feel. When we can express gratitude on a daily basis we have an emotional strength that pays off with greater energy and motivation.

Whether you have a large garden or a small one, you can increase your sense of satisfaction and happiness by expressing your gratitude silently or aloud. The following gratitude activity offers you an opportunity to increase your own happiness and life satisfaction.

Gratitude

Plan to spend five minutes each evening for the next two weeks on this practice. Prepare a pad of paper, a notebook, or a set of file cards and place them by your bed with a pen.

After you brush your teeth and get into bed, write up to five things in your life for which you are grateful. For instance, you might write such things as "waking up this morning," "coffee with a friend," "the shade of a tree," and "hearing my favorite song on the radio." As you can see from the examples, your gratitude list does not need to include only big, important events, but rather anything in the previous twenty-four hours that caused you to feel grateful.

Since this is a two-week exercise, wait until the two weeks are up to record your notes on the following page.

Notes

As the days went on, did it get easier or harder to think of things for your gratitude list? Over the two weeks, did you notice yourself looking at people, activities, or things any differently? Did you notice any change in your usual ways of feeling about things?

 ### Digging a Little Deeper

Think of someone in your life who currently lives somewhere nearby and who has had a positive impact on the person you have become and are becoming. This person might be a member of your family, a friend, or a colleague at work.

Write a thank-you letter to this person, expressing your gratitude. In the letter, remember specific times and incidents in which this person helped you. Your letter should be about one page in length.

Invite the person to spend some time with you, perhaps for coffee or for a meal. Don't tell them ahead of time what you plan to do as part of your time together, just that you'd like to see them.

It is important to deliver your appreciation face to face. In that way your gratefulness can move from your heart to theirs. During your shared time, begin reading your thank-you aloud, with expression and eye contact. Let the other person react. Enjoy remembering the events you shared.

You have completed the cycle! Just as there are possibilities for success and pleasure during every phase of gardening, there are also endless possibilities for enjoying the life process. In this section, you explored ways to celebrate more often in your daily life as well as ways to change your emotional 'soil' by moving your facial muscles. You also experienced the power of feeling successful by deciding your conditions of satisfaction before an interaction or event, and you looked at ways to build your own happiness quotient by the simple act of expressing gratitude.

What are your next steps? Do you want to do some redesigning? Perhaps you'd just like to weed and replant certain patches. Or maybe you want to sit back and enjoy the garden that is your life just as it is. The choice, as always, is yours.

Whether you decide to enjoy the garden of your life as it currently is or you want to redesign some parts, here are a few useful "growing yourself" instructions:

- Walk daily for at least 20 minutes, focusing your attention on your senses in the present moment.

- Journal each day, recording your thoughts and feelings.

- Sit quietly for at least 20 minutes daily, praying, reading, focusing on your breathing, or meditating.

- Daily spend time doing an activity that is personally satisfying to you.

- Take opportunities for daily reflection or go on a mini- or maxi- retreat to consider what you are currently doing and how it is aligned with the future you want.

Use your heightened awareness about ways to increase your success and pleasure during your day-to-day activities to design, plant, tend, and enjoy the life of your dreams!

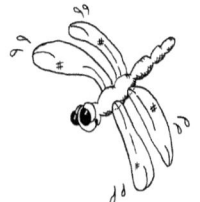

A Highly Selective List of Gardening Resources

The Garden Book: Designing, Creating, and Maintaining Your Garden, John Brookes, Penguin Books, Ltd., 1992
   A beautifully illustrated book of design.

The Garden Primer, Barbara Damrosch, Workman Publishing Co., 1988
   Comprehensive gardening information and advice.

The Organic Gardener's Handbook of Natural Pest and Disease Control: A Complete Problem-Solving Guide to Keeping Your Garden and Yard Healthy Without Chemicals, Barbara W. Ellis (Editor), Rodale Press, 1996
   An excellent reference book and diagnostic tool.

The Passion for Gardening, Ken Druse, Clarkson Porter, 2003
   A why-to garden book.

Right Plant, Right Place, Nicola Ferguson, Fireside, 1984
   An extensive plant selection guide.

The Rodale Book of Composting, Deborah L. Martin (Editor), Rodale Press, 1992
   All you ever wanted to know about composting.

The Well-Designed Mixed Garden: Building Beds & Borders with Trees, Shrubs, Perennials, Annuals, and Bulbs, Tracy DiSabato-Aust, Timber Press, 2003

Garden design fundamentals.

Western Garden Book, Kathleen Norris Brenzel (Editor), Sunset Publishing Co., 2001

The western U.S. gardener's bible.

An Equally Brief List of Personal Growth Resources

The Anatomy of Change, Richard Strozzi Heckler, North Atlantic Books, 1993
> Using the body's capacities to move through life transitions.

Authentic Happiness, Martin E. Seligman Ph.D., The Free Press. 2002
> Excellent practical wisdom about emotions.

Emotions Revealed, Paul Elman, Times Books, 2003
> How our emotions are signaled to others.

Finding Your Perfect Work, Paul and Sarah Edwards, Jeremy P. Tarcher/Putnam, 2003
> Hundreds of ideas about making a living doing what you love.

The Joy Diet, Martha Beck, Crown Publishers, 2003
> 10 ingredients for joy with commentary and exercises.

Mastery, George Leonard, Plume: Penguin Group, 1992
> A prescriptive guide to help you master anything you choose.

Repacking Your Bags, Richard Leider and David Shapiro, Berrett-Koehler, 2002
> Ways to lighten your load for the rest of your life.

Retooling On The Run, Stuart Heller and David Sheppard Surrenda, Frog, Ltd. 1994
> Strategies for turning ideas into action.

The Woman's Comfort Book, Jennifer Louden, Harper San Francisco, 1992
> A comprehensive resource for refreshing and replenishing the self.

You Are What You Say, Matthew Budd M.D. and Larry Rothstein, Crown, 2000
> A wonderfully insightful look into the way we use language to define our possibilities.

Your Money or Your Life, Joe Dominguez and Vicki Robin, Penguin, 1992
> The difference between making a living and making a life.

About Earthsong Voices

Earthsong Voices offers services and products to enrich your life or, as we like to say, fertilize the soul. We invite you to take one or more STEPs into our world:

Studios — At Earthsong Studios, C.L. Haney creates whimsical sketches and drawings to personalize books, greeting cards, and other printed material. She specializes in the delights of nature.

Treasures — From Earthsong Treasures, select a variety of items to grow with. Treasures may challenge your thinking or tickle your fancy. They also make great gifts.

Expressions — With Earthsong Expressions, Bonnie and C.L. provide personal growth books, workshops, and seminars. We customize for your group's needs.

Perspectives — Through Earthsong Perspectives, certified coach Bonnie Keast coaches individuals and small teams. Life balance and major life transitions, especially retirement, are her specialty.

About the Authors

BONNIE KEAST is a certified ontological and somatic coach with an Ed.D. in educational leadership. She lives in Northern California where she coaches individuals, teaches, and gives seminars on life transitions. Current dreams include swimming with dolphins and quietly watching a month of sunsets on a tropical island.

C.L. HANEY is an artist, illustrator, landscape designer, oenophile, and real estate consultant currently living in Southern Arizona. Tomorrow you may find her sketching her way around the world or painting in a sunlit cottage studio.

Bonnie and C.L. welcome your responses to *Cultivating The Garden Within*. Please contact them at *www.EarthsongVoices.com* to share your thoughts about the book and ways it helped you cultivate your personal soil. You may also use the website to request information about their seminars and workshops and to order additional copies of the book.

www.ingramcontent.com/pod-product-compliance
Lightning Source LLC
Chambersburg PA
CBHW071718090426
42738CB00009B/1810